Tilda the Builder

Maverick
Early Readers

'Tilda the Builder'
An original concept by Katie Dale
© Katie Dale 2021

Illustrated by Gisela Bohórquez

Published by MAVERICK ARTS PUBLISHING LTD

Studio 11, City Business Centre, 6 Brighton Road,

Horsham, West Sussex, RH13 5BB

© Maverick Arts Publishing Limited November 2021

+44 (0)1403 256941

A CIP catalogue record for this book is available at the British Library.

ISBN 978-1-84886-836-6

Maverick
publishing

www.maverickbooks.co.uk

Turquoise

This book is rated as: Turquoise Band (Guided Reading)

Tilda the Builder

by
Katie Dale

illustrated by
Gisela Bohórquez

Tilda loved to build things. She and her doggy pal, Buddy, could build anything. No job was too big or too small!

Every year, Tilda's town held a carnival.

There were lots of floats in all shapes and sizes.

Tilda and Buddy loved to help build them!

The baker had a cake-shaped float, the

fishmonger had a fish-shaped float, and the ice

cream shop's float looked like a giant ice cream!

But then, the day before the carnival...

CRACK!

The bridge broke!

"It must be the ghost!" the mayor cried.

"I always knew that bridge was haunted!

It always creaks when I drive over it, and

when I went swimming in the river the

ghost stole my ring!"

"Don't be silly," said his wife. "The bridge is old, that's all. You must have lost your ring."

"Well, ghost or no ghost, we can't hold the carnival if the bridge is broken!" the mayor sighed.

"Oh no!" everyone cried.

"Don't worry!" Tilda smiled. "Buddy and I will mend the bridge!"

Tilda brought some
new wood and
Buddy carried her
toolbox.

Tilda carefully measured
the wood.

Then she cut planks the right size.

But when she went to hammer the nails in...

...the pot of nails was missing!

"That's odd," Tilda said. "I must have left my nails at home! Come on, Buddy, let's go and get them!"

"Woof woof!" Buddy agreed.

But when Tilda tried to get in her van, her keys were missing!

Tilda frowned. "That's very odd! I had them a moment ago. Where could they be?"

Tilda and Buddy searched everywhere, but couldn't find the nails or her keys.

"Someone must have taken them," Tilda said, scratching her head.

"But who? We're the only people here." Tilda looked around at the empty riverbank. Then suddenly, she turned very pale.

"You don't think there really is a ghost, do you?" she asked Buddy.

Buddy whined and tried to hide behind Tilda's legs.

"Oh Buddy, what can we do?" Tilda wailed. "If we can't find my keys, we'll never fix the bridge in time for the carnival!"

"Woof!" Buddy barked, running over to Tilda's lunch bag.

"Good idea, let's eat some lunch," Tilda said.

"Brain food will help us solve the problem."

Buddy wagged his tail. Eating always cheered him up!

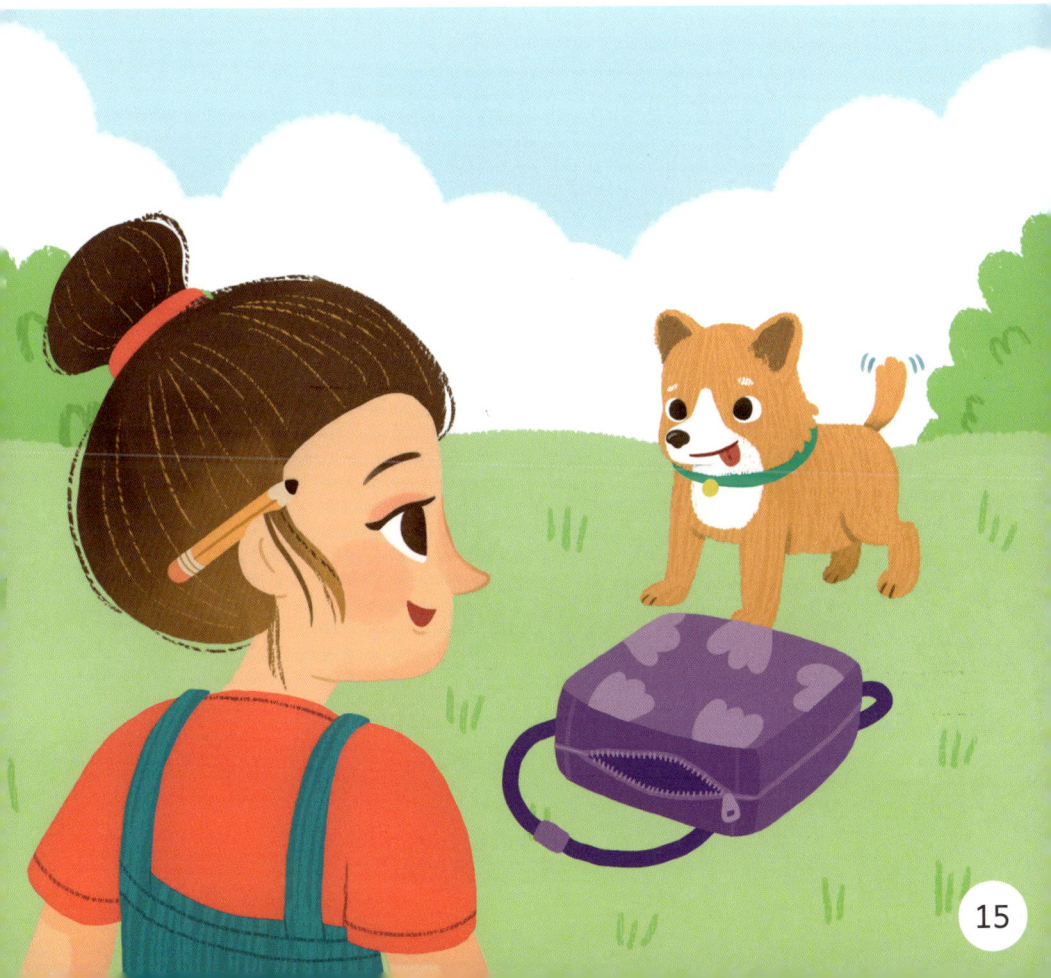

But when Tilda went to get her sandwiches, she got a shock. The tin foil packet was open, and the sandwiches were half-eaten!

"How very odd!" Tilda gasped. "Ghosts don't eat sandwiches! What is going on?"

Buddy sniffed at the tin foil – then suddenly he ran away into the trees!

"Buddy, come back!" Tilda cried. "I can't lose you too!"

Tilda ran after Buddy and found him barking up at a tree.

"What is it, boy?" she asked, looking up into the branches. Suddenly she spotted something glinting in the sunlight.

"Is that... it can't be!"

Tilda gasped. "It is! It's my keys!"

Tilda's van keys were hanging from a branch in the tree!

"How did they get up there?!" said Tilda.

Tilda fetched her ladder and climbed up to get her keys. But as she got to the top, she had a big surprise.

"Buddy, there are LOTS of strange things up here!" she gasped. "There's tin foil, coins, a ring – and my pot of nails! It must be a magpie nest! They love to steal shiny things!"

Just then, a magpie fluttered down onto a nearby branch.

"Squawk!" it cried crossly as Tilda took the shiny things out of its nest.

"I'm sorry," Tilda said. "But these things don't belong to you.

The magpie looked sad.

"Here, have half my sandwich instead,"

Tilda smiled, putting it in the nest.

"Squawk!" the magpie cried happily,

eating the sandwich greedily.

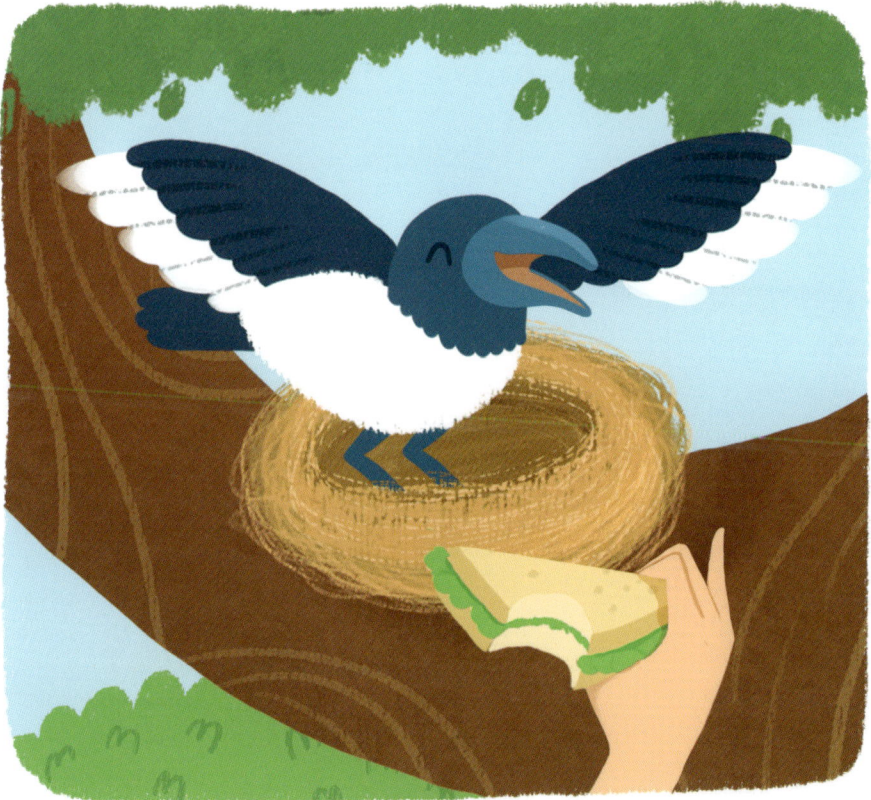

Finally, Tilda finished mending the bridge.

"Thank you so much, Tilda!" the mayor cried.

"Happy to help!" Tilda smiled. "And we found your ring!"

"You mean, it wasn't taken by a ghost?"

he gasped.

"No ghosts!" Tilda smiled. "Just a very

cheeky magpie!"

"Phew!" the mayor grinned. "Thank you so much, Tilda! Now the carnival can go ahead after all!"

"Hurray!" Tilda beamed.

"Woof! Woof!" Buddy barked, wagging his tail.

On the day of the carnival, everyone cheered and waved as the floats went past. All of the floats looked amazing!

But when Tilda and Buddy came past, they got the biggest cheer of all!

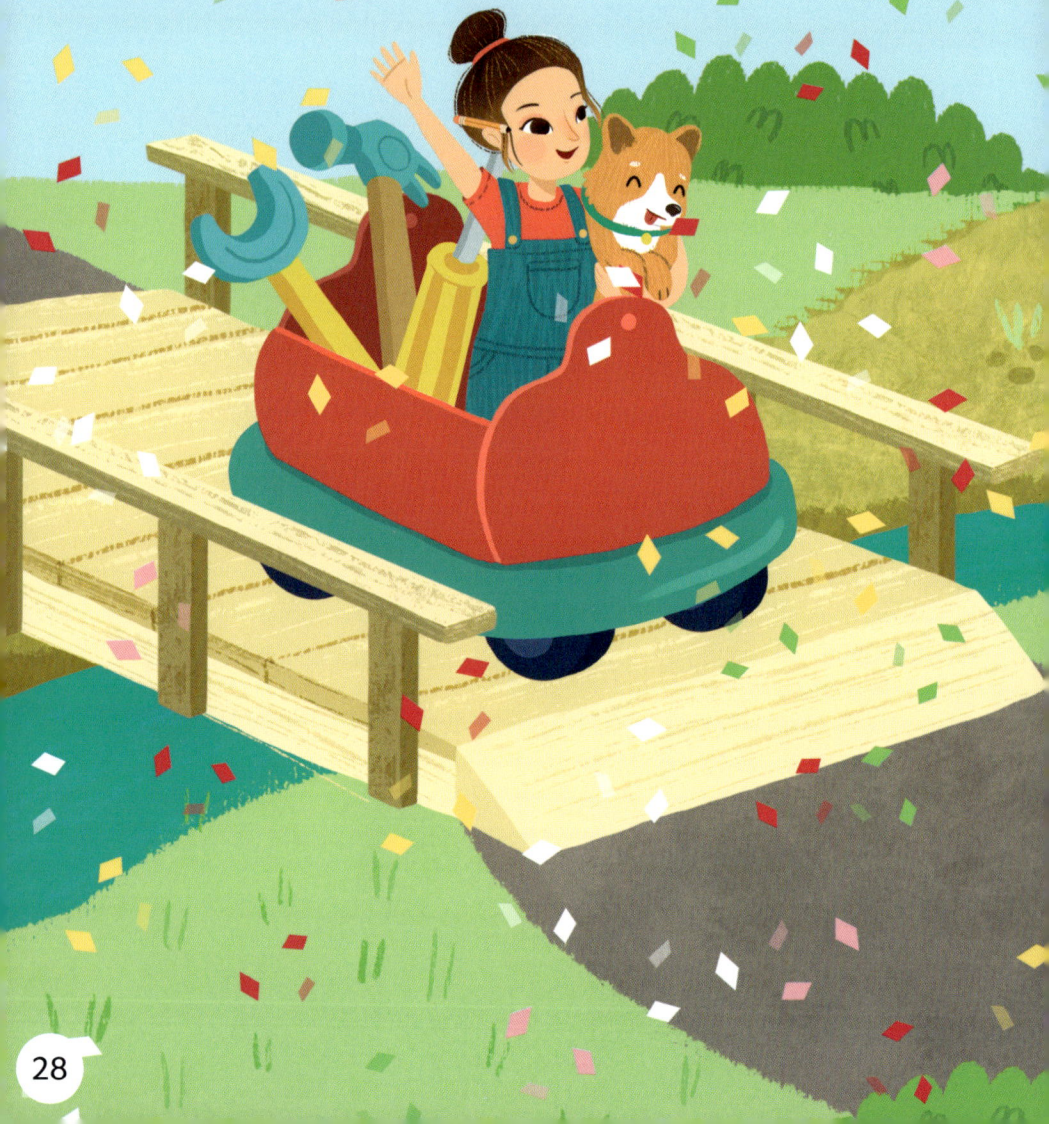

Quiz

1. What happened the day before the carnival?
a) Tilda got sick
b) The bridge broke
c) A float broke

2. What did the mayor lose?
a) A ring
b) A necklace
c) A coin

3. What was Tilda looking for?
a) Coins and tin foil
b) Nails and keys
c) A hammer and spanner

4. Where did Tilda find her keys?
a) Hanging from a branch
b) In her toolbox
c) In a nest

5. What had taken all of the shiny things?
a) A crow
b) A seagull
c) A magpie

Turn over for answers

Book Bands for Guided Reading

The Institute of Education book banding system is a scale of colours that reflects the various levels of reading difficulty. The bands are assigned by taking into account the content, the language style, the layout and phonics. Word, phrase and sentence level work is also taken into consideration.

Maverick Early Readers are a bright, attractive range of books covering the pink to white bands. All of these books have been book banded for guided reading to the industry standard and edited by a leading educational consultant.

Pink

Red

Yellow

Blue

Green

Orange

Turquoise

Purple

Gold

White

To view the whole Maverick Readers scheme, visit our website at
www.maverickearlyreaders.com

Or scan the QR code above to view our scheme instantly!

Quiz Answers: 1b, 2a, 3b, 4a, 5c